When I grow up, I want to...

Look After the Planet

NoodleJUICE

Noodle Juice Ltd

www.noodle-juice.com

Stonesfield House, Stanwell Lane, Great Bourton, Oxfordshire, OX17 1QS

First published in Great Britain 2023

Copyright © Noodle Juice Ltd 2023

Text by Noodle Juice 2022

Illustrations by Flavio Remontti 2022

Printed in China

A CIP catalogue record of this book is available from the British Library.

ISBN: 978-1-915613-06-6

13 5 7 9 10 8 6 4 2

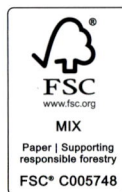

FSC
www.fsc.org
MIX
Paper | Supporting responsible forestry
FSC® C005748

This book is made from FSC®-certified paper. By choosing this book, you help to take care of the world's forests. Learn more: www.fsc.org.

Contents

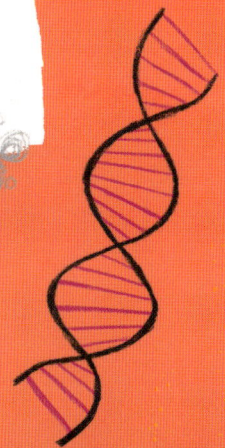

This is a scientist.

Scientists study the world around us and work out how to **make things better**.

The goal of a scientist is to add knowledge to the world and sometimes to make **new discoveries** or inventions.

They use strict scientific rules to make sure their results are **factually accurate**.

Scientists work in medicine, **climate change**, energy, food and technology. They study space, metals, the Earth and the sea, as well as humans.

Scientists are **experts**.

Scientists are very important because they find solutions to problems and **improve our lives**.

CERTIFICATE

CERTIFICATE

Scientists help to look after the planet.

This is a zookeeper.

A zookeeper helps to look after animals that may be **extinct** in the wild.

By caring for animals in **captivity**, zookeepers are able to study them more closely.

Zoos are good places to educate families about **animal conservation**.

SO CUTE!

Zookeepers help to **raise funds** to support research projects across the world.

Zookeepers always try to **recycle or reuse** everything they can.

Some zoos have **breeding programmes** to make sure that animals are able to have babies.

Zookeepers help to look after the planet.

This is a journalist.

A journalist's role is to report what is happening in the world **accurately**.

DAILY NEWS

Journalists can write in **newspapers** or **online**. They can appear on radio programmes or on television.

BREAKING NEWS

TV

TV

Some journalists focus on issues such as **climate change** or human rights.

VOTE for ME!

Other journalists concentrate on **politics** and make sure that people understand what is happening.

They make sure that the news that they report is correct.

Journalists often travel to report their stories and sometimes need a **photographer** too.

Without journalists, we would be **unaware** of issues that might affect us or our world.

Journalists help to look after the planet.

This is a recycling expert.

A recycling expert encourages people at home and at work to **recycle** as much rubbish as possible.

REDUCE! REUSE! RECYCLE!

They make sure that recycling banks are **emptied** regularly.

RECYCLING IS THE FUTURE

A recycling expert understands what **materials** can be reused and who will want to use them.

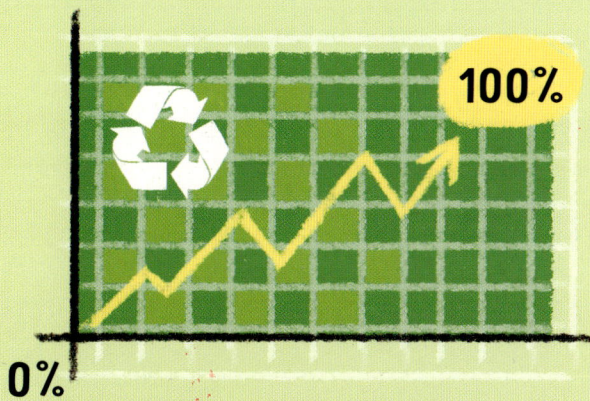

They visit schools to teach children how **important** recycling is.

Some recycling experts work in business and help their colleagues reach **net zero** carbon emissions.

CO_2

Zero!

A recycling expert helps us to reach the government's recycling **targets**.

0%

100%

Recycling experts help to look after the planet.

This is a landscape designer.

Landscape designers create amazing **outdoor spaces** for homeowners, businesses, schools and other organisations.

They work with **plants**, and materials such as stone or wood, to make open air spaces functional and inviting for their clients.

Planting trees and shrubs helps to reduce **noise pollution** and provide shade.

By planting insect friendly plants, landscape designers can provide **habitats** for endangered species.

They also work with engineers to help create **flood defences.**

Some landscape designers work for towns and cities and are responsible for making **public spaces** a pleasure to spend time in.

Landscape designers help to look after the planet.

This is a wildlife rescuer.

Wildlife rescuers help to look after **hurt** or orphaned wild animals.

They often work with vets to make sure that the animals will be happy and healthy when they are **returned** to the wild.

A rescuer will need to **feed, clean and treat** the animals in their care.

Some rescuers work in zoos or **aquariums**. Others might look after birds or sea mammals in the wild.

Sometimes animals need rescuing from things that humans have caused, such as an **oil spill**.

Educating the public is an important part of a wildlife rescuer's job.

Wildlife rescuers help to look after the planet.

This is a marine scientist.

A marine scientist studies the **sea** and the sea creatures and plants that live in it.

They study all parts of the sea, including **coral reefs**, icebergs, the ocean floor and sea water itself.

Marine scientists record information about the sea so that they can identify when things **change**.

SALT

Some marine scientists focus on how much **salt** is in the sea. If the amount grows or shrinks too much, it can affect the climate.

Other scientists study how sea creatures interact with each other. If krill start to die off, then many **whales** won't have enough food.

71%

HUNGRY!

As the sea covers 71% of the planet, marine scientists are important as they help to **protect** that environment.

Marine scientists help to look after the planet.

This is a forester.

A forester looks after trees in **woodlands** and forests.

Trees are important because they give us oxygen and store **carbon**. They also provide homes for the world's wildlife.

HEIGHT ☑
WIDTH ☑

Foresters need to **survey** the trees in their woodlands, looking for signs of ill health or damaged trunks or branches.

Keeping a woodland healthy requires foresters to spend a lot of time **working outside**.

A forester will plant **new** trees to replace the ones felled for wood. They choose the best tree species for their woodlands.

Some foresters work for the **charities** who own many of our forests, so that we can enjoy them.

Foresters help to look after the planet.

19

This is a planet engineer.

Planet engineers study the world, looking for ways to improve the Earth's environment.

They are very focused on how to reduce the impact of climate change.

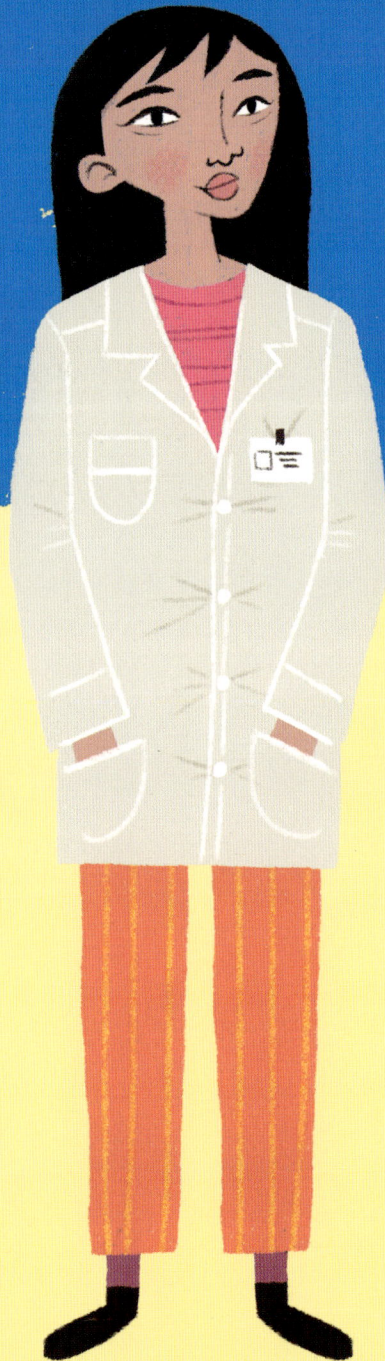

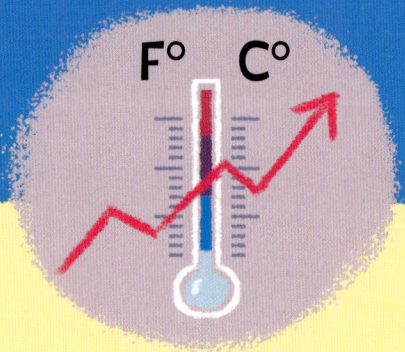

F° C°

They develop **new technologies** that can help improve our world.

SAVE THE EARTH!

HA! HA! HA!

YOU FAILED.

These projects are very big and can often seem like **science fiction**. Some ideas include a space mirror to reflect the Sun's energy or mining asteroids for precious metals.

They also look at ways to remove carbon dioxide from the atmosphere, such as planting **millions** of trees.

Planet engineers also study other planets to see if they could create a liveable **habitat** on another world.

Planet engineers help to look after the planet.

This is an eco teacher.

Eco teachers work in schools, museums and national parks to teach us about **ecology**.

Welcome
NATIONAL PARK

Ecology is the study of how all living things **connect** with each other and their environment.

An eco teacher needs to know about **biology, chemistry, physics and geology**.

They may also run research projects to find out how **natural habitats** are affected by man-made issues, such as pollution.

Eco teachers create **educational resources** for schools, families and people who visit places of environmental interest.

They may also give talks or **guided walks** that teach people about the world around them.

Eco teachers help to look after the planet.

This is a weather scientist.

Weather scientists collect and study information about the **atmosphere**.

Another name for weather scientists is **meteorologists**.

Meteorologists collect data from **satellite images**, weather stations and other sensors, and use it to tell us what the weather will be like.

SALE

SALE

Some weather scientists forecast weather for customers, such as supermarkets, so they know when to have their BBQ sausages ready for sale.

Others study weather patterns to predict **floods** and droughts.

Weather scientists also study how the weather can affect the spread of **pollution or disease**.

Weather scientists help to look after the planet.

This is a food scientist.

Food scientists study the food we eat to make sure it is **safe**.

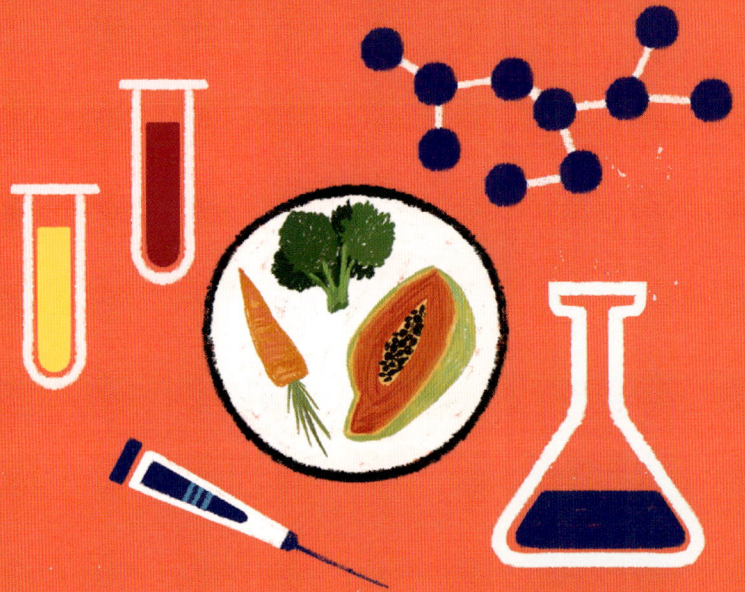

Food scientists look at the **nutritional value** of our food and work out what we should eat to stay healthy.

Food scientists also invent **new flavours and recipes**, making sure our food stays fresh for longer.

They improve crops, such as wheat, to make them more **resistant** to pests.

Some food scientists work with **farmers** to help them grow more food from their land.

Others work with the **World Health Organisation** to support countries suffering from flooding or drought.

Food scientists help to look after the planet.

This is a conservationist.

Conservationists look after the natural world to make sure that humans don't **destroy it**.

They want to understand how **humans**, wildlife and the natural world affect each other.

Conservationists record information, such as the **number** of different animals present in an area, or what might be in the soil.

They help to **protect** animals, plants and their natural habitats.

Part of their role is to show us how to live **sustainably** and increase the numbers of different plants and animals in the world.

POISON

DONATE TODAY

NATURE

TREES

WHALES

SAVE THE WILDLIFE!

OCEANS

They also help to **raise money** to support conservation projects.

Conservationists help to look after the planet.

There are so many different ways to look after the planet.

Food scientist

Conservationist

Scientist

Eco teacher

Recycling expert

Weather scientist

Journalist

Planet engineer

Forester

Wildlife rescuer

Marine scientist

Zookeeper

Landscape designer

Which one will you choose?

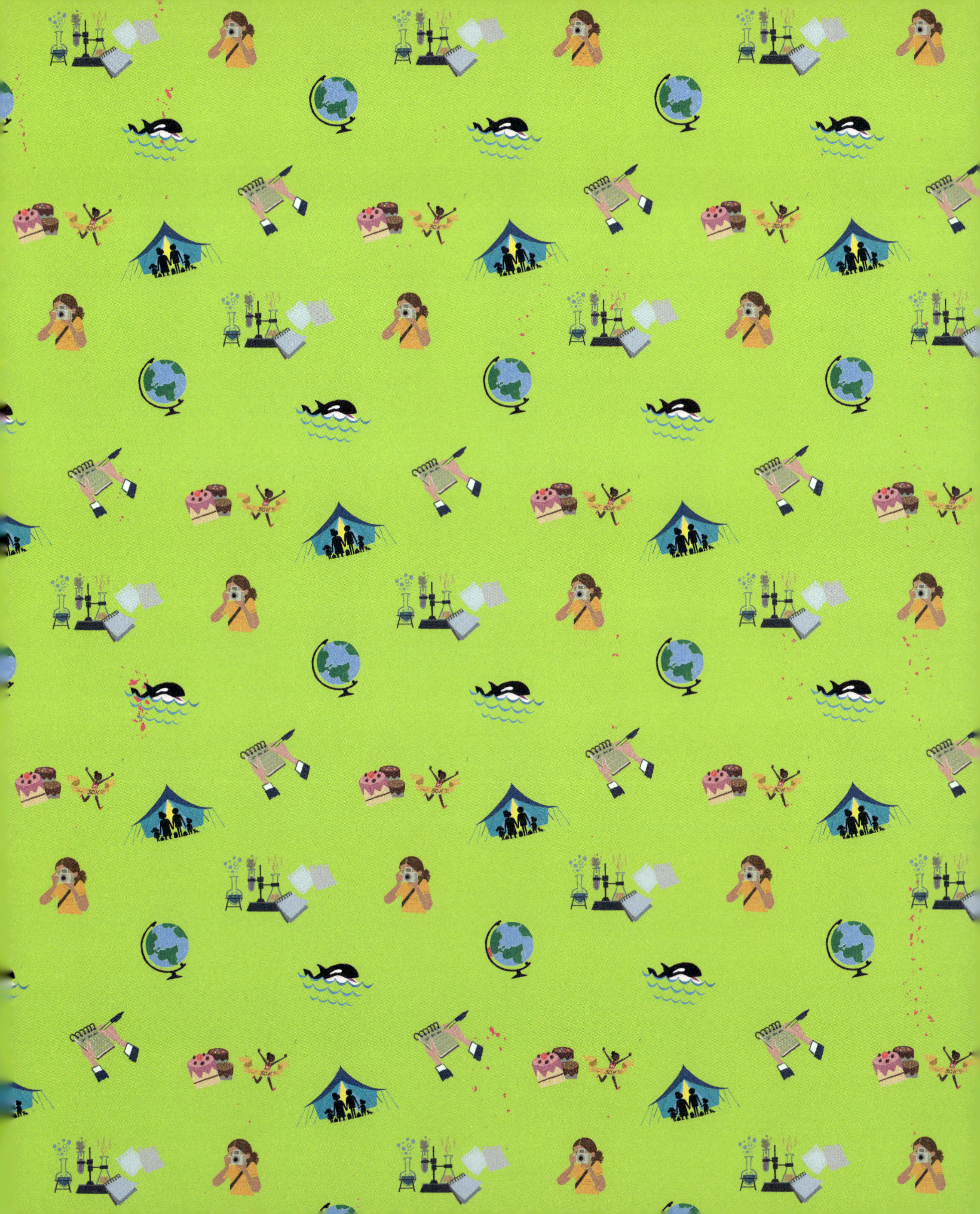